This journal belongs to

....

My grandchildren call me

....

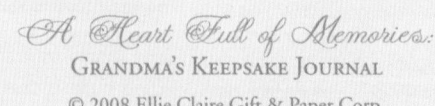

A Heart Full of Memories:
GRANDMA'S KEEPSAKE JOURNAL

© 2008 Ellie Claire Gift & Paper Corp.
www.ellieclaire.com

Compiled by Barbara Farmer
Designed by Lisa & Jeff Franke

Scripture references are from the following sources: The Holy Bible, New International Version® NIV®.
© 1973, 1978, 1984 by International Bible Society. Used by permission of Zondervan. The New King James
Version (NKJV). Copyright © 1982 by Thomas Nelson, Inc. Used by permission. The Living Bible (TLB)
copyright © 1971 by permission of Tyndale House Publishers, Inc., Wheaton, IL. The Message. © 1993, 1994,
1995, 1996, 2000, 2001, 2002 by Eugene Peterson. Used by permission of NavPress, Colorado Springs, CO.
The Holy Bible, New Living Translation (NLT) copyright © 1996, 2004. Used by permission of Tyndale
House Publishers, Inc., Wheaton, IL. www.newlivingtranslation.com. The New Century Version® (NCV).
Copyright © 1987, 1988, 1991 by Thomas Nelson, Inc. Used by permission. All rights reserved.

ISBN 978-1-934770-29-0
Printed in China

A HEART FULL OF

Memories

GRANDMA'S KEEPSAKE
JOURNAL

Ellie Claire
gift & paper expressions

...inspired by life

Grandma's Family....

Great-Grandfather

Grandfather

Great-Grandmother

Father

Great-Grandfather

Grandmother

Great-Grandmother

Grandma

Great-Grandfather

Grandfather

Great-Grandmother

Mother

Great-Grandfather

Grandmother

Great-Grandmother

Grandpa's Family....

Great-Grandfather

Grandfather

Great-Grandmother

Father

Great-Grandfather

Grandmother

Great-Grandmother

Grandpa

Great-Grandfather

Grandfather

Great-Grandmother

Mother

Great-Grandfather

Grandmother

Great-Grandmother

Forward

I have a box of journals my Grandmother kept at their summer cabin. She would use them to describe the day, tell who came to visit, record how many fish were caught, and jot down incidental stories. These are a treasure to me—an heirloom. She came to mind often while compiling this book.

Some grandmas could pick up a pen and fill a journal with ease, while others may feel they don't know where to start. But *every grandchild knows* their grandma has something to share with them.

Let this book be a guide to sharing your treasures with the ones you love. Take a look inside. It's filled with encouragement and inspiration. There are no fill-in-the-blanks. Instead there is lightly suggested ideas within topical sections that will gently guide your thoughts and memories. Follow along or write right over the top of them. Draw pictures, write poems, paste photos; it's up to you. Take your time and enjoy sharing it even before it's all filled up.

You've lived, learned, laughed, loved, and made a heart full of memories. *Grandma's Keepsake Journal* will help you share them.

FROM THE EDITOR

Our Heritage

These are the children
God has given me.
God has been good to me.

GENESIS 33:5 NCV

In the midst of the praying, it is comforting
to remember that God considers families important.
Before He called a nation, He created a family.

QUIN SHERRER

Our nationalities....

Exploring our roots....

Coming to America....

Cultures and Customs we brought
with us....

Transitions through
generations....

Languages spoken....

Who's Who in our family....

Your ancestor was famous for....

Did you know you are related to....

He was known for....

She was famous because...

*C*hildren's children are a crown to the aged,
and parents are the pride of their children.

PROVERBS 17:6 NIV

Heavenly Father, Thank You for the unique personalities that You have given to each and every child. Help me to discover each talent and gift with which You have blessed my children, and may I learn how to best cultivate each of the blossoms You have planted within their souls. Amen.

KIM BOYCE

It's in the genes....

We all have the same—
nose...eyes...ears...hair...height....

It seems we all like....

We share some similar talents....

The family business....

We have a flair for....

Family reunions....

Visiting the Old Country....

Connecting with distant relatives...

Events with the whole family...

It takes wisdom to have a good family, and it takes
understanding to make it strong.

PROVERBS 24:3 NCV

Tell the next generation detail by detail the story of God, our God forever, who guides us till the end of time.

PSALM 48:14 THE MESSAGE

Stories about your family....

Let me tell you what your mom used to do....

You'll never believe what
your dad did....

Family traditions....

Holiday celebrations....

Passing on legacies....

Heirlooms the family has collected....

Grandmas should write down the stories of their lives, however dull they seem to them. For such tales show history as it is— a procession of interlocking lives. A unity. The family of mankind.

CHARLOTTE GRAY

My Childhood

How dear to the heart are the
scenes of my childhood, when fond
recollection presents them to view.

SAMUEL WOODWORTH

Count your nights by stars, not shadows.
Count your days by smiles, not tears.
And on any birthday morning,
count your age by friends, not years.

My birthplace....

Date & Time....

Weight & Length...

Distinguishing marks....

Family resemblance....

The best part of growing up was....

*I still remember the feeling
I had when....*

*The best of times,
the worst of times....*

What I hoped for....

I still hope for....

My favorite childhood memory....

ow we hope for the blessings God has for His children.
These blessings, which cannot be destroyed or be spoiled
or lose their beauty, are kept in heaven for you.

1 PETER 1:4 NCV

We shared. Parents. Home. Pets. Celebrations. Catastrophes. Secrets.
And the threads of our experience became so interwoven that we are linked.
I can never be utterly lonely, knowing you share the planet.

PAMELA BROWN

My siblings....

Our birth order....

We stuck together through
thick and thin....

Sibling rivalry....

I shared a room with....

Where I grew up....

We lived near....

It took so long to get to....

Our favorite hangout was....

I remember when we would....

_____

_____

_____

_____

Every Saturday night we....

_____

_____

_____

*A special treat for
our family was....*

_____

_____

When I was a child, I spoke and thought and reasoned as a child.
But when I grew up, I put away childish things.

1 CORINTHIANS 13:11 NLT

We all belong to another world, to another time, to another place of long ago. I believe it is important to share your history with those you love so that they will be able to tell their children about the foundation of their lives.

CHRISTOPHER DE VINCK

Living history....

I'll never forget when....

I heard the news while I was....

My heart felt like...

I couldn't help thinking....

My parents taught me....

I'll never forget what
Mama said....

Daddy's advice was....

*My own grandmother
told me....*

*C*hildren who obey what they have been taught are wise.

PROVERBS 28:7 NCV

I applied my heart to what I observed and learned a lesson from what I saw.

PROVERBS 24:32 NIV

If I could go back....

The lesson I learned....

How my choices impact me still today....

I knew I was all
grown up when....

Changing my views....

Then and now....

Adventures, Milestones, Events

There is nothing...more wholesome and useful for life in later years than some good memory, especially a memory connected with childhood, with home.

FYODOR DOSTOYEVSKY

Exploring my own backyard....

The neighborhood gang....

Discovering our world....

Finding new friends....

We throw open our doors to God and discover at the same moment
that He has already thrown open His door to us. We find ourselves
standing where we always hoped...out in the wide open spaces of God's
grace and glory, standing tall and shouting our praise.

ROMANS 5:2 THE MESSAGE

The world is not a playground, it is a schoolroom.
Life is not a holiday, but an education.
And the one eternal lesson for us all is how better we can love.

HENRY DRUMMOND

School days....

My High School....

My favorite activity....

My sport was....

My best friend was....

My first crush....

Celebrating major achievements....

Learning to drive....

The first job I had was....

My first paycheck!...

Going on my first date...

We're rooting for the truth to win out in you. We...celebrate
every strength, every triumph of the truth in you.
We pray hard that it will all come together in your lives.

2 CORINTHIANS 13:8-9 THE MESSAGE

Some of the most rewarding and beautiful moments of a friendship happen in the unforeseen open spaces between planned activities.

CHRISTINE LEEFELDT

My favorite place to hang out....

Youth groups and church activities....

I was a member of....

My senior year....

My favorite subject was....

There was this great teacher....

I was inspired by....

Graduation day!....

*G*o forth seeking adventure. Open your eyes, your ears, your mind,
your heart, your spirit and you'll find adventure everywhere.

WILFERD A. PETERSON

"For I know the plans I have for you," declares the Lord, "plans to prosper you and not to harm you, plans to give you hope and a future."

JEREMIAH 29:11 NIV

My future plans were....

Heading out into
the world....

Living on my own....

What I learned
along the way.....

Whatever you do, don't....

Never miss the opportunity to....

*S*o be very careful how you live. Do not live like those who are not wise,
but live wisely. Use every chance you have for doing good.

EPHESIANS 5:15-16 NCV

All About Me and Grandpa

Love...it begins with a moment
that grows richer and brighter...
and becomes a lifetime of joy.

Love is patient and kind. Love is not jealous or boastful or proud or rude....
Love never gives up, never loses faith, is always hopeful,
and endures through every circumstance.

1 CORINTHIANS 13:4, 7 NLT

The first time I saw him....

First impressions....

He asked me out....

We had our first date....

Our courtship....

The first kiss....

We knew it was love....

Enjoying time together....

He popped the question....

We spread the news....

The date was set...

So many plans to make...

I wish I could tell you the day, the hour, the minute my love for you became real. I only know it seems I've loved you forever.

For this reason man will leave his father and mother and is united to his wife, and they will become one flesh.

GENESIS 2:24 NIV

Our wedding day:

The date....

The place....

The time....

The season...

The weather...

Something old—
something new...

Something borrowed—
something blue....

Wedding Day Memories....

The wedding party....

The ceremony....

Mr. & Mrs....

The reception....

Remembering special guests....

A funny thing happened....

Line by line, moment by moment, special times are etched into our memories in the permanent ink of everlasting love in our relationships.

GLORIA GAITHER

Out of respect for Christ, be courteously reverent to one another.
Wives, understand and support your husbands....
Husbands, go all out in your love for your wives.

EPHESIANS 5:21-22, 25 THE MESSAGE

Our get-away car....

Heading out on our own....

Our honeymoon spot....

Plans for the future....

*Coming back home and
setting up house....*

Milestone memories....

Our children are born....

Buying our first home....

Special anniversaries....

Significant trips we've taken....

Places we dreamed of visiting...

When the first time of love is over, there comes a something better still.
Then comes that other love; that faithful friendship which never changes,
and which will accompany you with its calm life through the whole of life.

FREDRIKA BREMER

Take nothing for granted. Stay wide-awake in prayer.
Most of all, love each other as if your life depended on it.
Love makes up for practically anything.

1 Peter 4:7-8 the message

Our Song....

Quiet times together....

Our favorite place to go on a date....

Special friends through the years....

Our stories and
adventures together....

There was that one
special memory....

Who Am I

Recognizing who we are in Christ and aligning our life with God's purpose for us gives a sense of destiny.... It gives form and direction to our life.

JEAN FLEMING

My spiritual gifts are....

I would say my special talent is....

There were so many ways to share....

How my life changed when I found my niche....

There are different kinds of spiritual gifts, but the same Spirit is the source of them all.... A spiritual gift is given to each of us so we can help each other.

1 CORINTHIANS 12:4, 7 NLT

Is it so small a thing to have enjoyed the sun, to have lived light in the spring, to have loved, to have thought, to have done?

MATTHEW ARNOLD

An activity I especially love to do....

My hobbies were....

When ever I'd get the chance,
I would....

But I really dislike to do....

My hopes and dreams
for myself are....

I am still learning....

There are so many things
I still want to do....

Always respect the Lord. Then you will have hope for the future,
and your wishes will come true.

PROVERBS 23:17-18 NCV

The reflective life is a life that is attentive, receptive, and responsive to what God is doing in us and around us. It's a life that asks God to reach into our heart, allowing Him to touch us there.

KEN GIRE

What touches my heart most of all is....

I can't help but cry when....

It makes me laugh
so hard when....

The scariest thing
I know is....

My temper flares when....

I treasure time spent....

*The most important
things in my life....*

"Heirlooms" I want to pass on to my children and grandchildren....

Do not lay up for yourselves treasures on earth...but lay up for yourselves treasures in heaven.... For where your treasure is, there your heart will be also.

MATTHEW 6:19-21 NKJV

We are each a secret to the other. To know one another means to feel mutual affection and confidence, and to believe in one another.

ALBERT SCHWEITZER

Something special about me that nobody knew before....

You'll never guess my
secret strength....

The mysterious
side of me...

I feel very blessed because....

I was surprised by this blessing....

*How I want to share
my blessings....*

The Lord will give strength to His people;
the Lord will bless His people with peace.

PSALM 29:11 NKJV

My Faith
in God

Faith isn't the ability to believe
long and far into the misty future.
It's simply taking God at His
word and taking the next step.

JONI EARECKSON TADA

May the Lord lead your hearts into a full understanding and expression of the love of God and the patient endurance that comes from Christ.

2 THESSALONIANS 3:5 NLT

God caught my attention when....

My first knowledge of God was....

*God revealed His
love to me by....*

There was this special person
who taught me about God....

My main influence
to believe was....

God's love was expressed
to me when...

Who we are is connected to those we love and to those who have influenced us toward goodness.

CHRISTOPHER DE VINCK

As you received Christ Jesus the Lord, so continue to live in Him. Keep your roots deep in Him and have your lives built on Him.

COLOSSIANS 2:6-7 NCV

I accepted Christ when....

The day I believed....

*My life changed in
so many ways....*

I had to tell somebody....

God showed His
faithfulness to me....

Even when times
were tough, I felt....

When I was alone,
God would....

Drawing closer to Him....

The everlasting arms are beneath us; we shall be caught, rescued, restored.
This is God's promise; this is how good He is.

J. I. PACKER

Ask, and it will be given to you; seek, and you will find; knock, and it will be opened to you. For everyone who asks receives, and he who seeks finds, and to him who knocks it will be opened.

MATTHEW 7:7-8 NKJV

Answers to Prayer....

When I called out to Him....

My prayer partners....

My favorite time and way to pray....

Grateful Thoughts and Praises....

I can't thank you enough, Lord....

What joy I have
in you, God....

To be grateful is to recognize the Love of God in everything He has given us—and He has given us everything. Every breath we draw is a gift of His love, every moment of existence is a gift of grace.

THOMAS MERTON

Anyone who believes in the Son of God has this testimony in his heart.... And this is the testimony: God has given us eternal life, and this life is in His Son. He who has the Son has life.

1 JOHN 5:10-12 NIV

My testimony....

How the Spirit moved in me....

I'll never forget how God
used me when....

I pray for your testimony....

Becoming a Mother

A mother's heart is always with her children.

We're going to have a baby! ...

All the advice I was given....

Oh, those maternity clothes....

Shopping for baby....

*Y*ou created my inmost being; You knit me
together in my mother's womb.

PSALM 139:13 NIV

Behold, children are a heritage from the Lord,
the fruit of the womb is a reward.

PSALM 127:3 NKJV

Time to go to the hospital....

Getting there on time....

Delivery ward stories....

Giving birth then was
so different...

...but in so many ways
still the same...

All my Children's names....

Special meanings
and origins....

Connections to other relatives....

Resemblances....

When we first bend over the cradle of our own child,
God throws back the temple door and reveals to us the sacredness
and mystery of our father's and mother's love to ourselves.

HENRY WARD BEECHER

$\mathcal{L}$et the little children come to Me, and do not forbid them;
for of such is the kingdom of God.

MARK 10:14 NKJV

*A prayer I prayed when
each child was born....*

Memories I pondered
in my heart....

Oh, what joy....

A time to bond....

Siblings meeting new siblings....

*Funny things kids say
about babies....*

I feel from a spiritual standpoint that there's a real celebration of
humanity, of the common bond of everybody. We need each other.

AMY GRANT

If you...know how to give good gifts to your children, how much more will your Father who is in heaven give good things to those who ask Him!

MATTHEW 7:11 NKJV

Showers and celebrations....

Friends and family
who visited....

Special gifts and heirlooms....

Stories about my children....

Getting into trouble....

Talking their way out of trouble....

Having fun with their imaginations....

What do you do when there is no television....

Father, help me to take the time to create stories with my children.
May good memories hold the generations together.

SCOTT WALKER

Becoming
a Grandma

If becoming a grandmother was
only a matter of choice I should advise
every one of you straight away to become
one. There is no fun for old people like it!

HANNAH WHITALL SMITH

Grandmother was sitting in a low rocking-chair, with the baby
in her arms, bending over it with eyes of worship.

LAURA E. RICHARDS

*My first thoughts when I was
told I would become a grandma....*

You should have seen how proud Grandpa was....

All your beautiful names....

Each name has a
special meaning....

*Family names
passed down...*

$\mathscr{A}$ good name is to be chosen rather than great riches,
loving favor rather than silver and gold.

PROVERBS 22:1 NKJV

A cheerful look brings joy to the heart,
and good news gives health to the bones.

PROVERBS 15:30 NIV

The special day arrived....

How we heard the news....

Every birthday has a story....

You remind me of....

Play time!....

All the fun we have together....

Our favorite games....

We used to love to....

Those gasps of astonishment, those shrieks of pleasure, those sighs of delight, lost long ago when your children grew wise and worldly, are suddenly given back to you by your grandchildren.

PAMELA BROWN

I have not stopped thanking God for you. I pray for you constantly, asking God...to give you spiritual wisdom and insight so that you might grow in your knowledge of God.

EPHESIANS 1:16-17 NLT

What an inspiration you are....

You were in my heart before
you were even in my arms....

You should see Grandpa!....

He was so proud....

You liked to call him....

*Special moments
with Grandpa....*

*O*ne of the most powerful handclasps is that of a new grandbaby
around the finger of a grandfather.

JOY HARGROVE

*Let me proclaim Your power to this new generation,
Your mighty miracles to all who come after me.*

PSALM 71:18 NLT

I will pray for you....

You can call me anytime....

I'm always here for you....

If you need a listening ear....

Role Models and Influences

Whatever is true, whatever is noble, whatever is right, whatever is pure, whatever is lovely, whatever is admirable—if anything is excellent or praiseworthy— think about such things.

PHILIPPIANS 4:8 NIV

There was this special friend....

What an impression
she made....

She really impacted my life....

A true friend inspires you to believe the best in yourself, to keep pursuing your deepest dreams—most wonderful of all, she celebrates all your successes as if they were her own!

Make sure you stay alert. Keep close watch over yourselves....
Don't let your heart wander off. Stay vigilant as long as you live.
Teach what you've seen and heard to your children and grandchildren.

DEUTERONOMY 4:9 THE MESSAGE

My Grandma taught
me so much...

I'll never forget the influence
my Grandpa had on me....

_Other family and friends who
shared so much with me...._

My teacher made such an
impact on my life....

That was an amazing year....

*What I discovered in
that classroom....*

The best teachers teach from the heart, not from the book.

CAROL JOHNSTON

*Nurture your mind with great thoughts;
to believe in the heroic makes heroes.*

BENJAMIN DISRAELI

My favorite childhood hero was....

I would emulate them by....

My heroes now are....

The characteristics I
admire most in them....

How I try to emulate them....

I read this book that affected
me so much....

The author was so good at....

My perspective has changed....

My favorite author...

....

....

....

Fiction...

....

....

Non-fiction and Biographies...

....

....

Classics...

....

....

Let us pursue the things which make for peace and the things
by which one may edify another.

ROMANS 14:19 NKJV

If there is a God who speaks anywhere, surely He speaks here: through waking up and working, through going away and coming back again, through people you read and books you meet, through falling asleep in the dark.

FREDERICK BUECHNER

The greatest movie
I ever saw....

That play made such
an impression....

Ah..the theater....

*Stories that caught
my attention....*

An event that forever
changed my existence....

Where it happened....

Where I was when
it happened....

How I felt....

*What changed in my
life because of it....*

Do not be shaped by this world; instead be changed within by a new way
of thinking. Then you will be able to decide what God wants for you.

ROMANS 12:2 NCV

Advice
and
Wisdom

*Wisdom is sweet to your soul;
if you find it, there is a future hope for you,
and your hope will not be cut off.*

PROVERBS 24:14 NIV

It is easy in the world to live after the world's opinion...it is easy, in solitude, after our own; but the great man is he who, in the midst of the crowd, keeps with perfect sweetness the independence of solitude.

RALPH WALDO EMERSON

The world is full of opinions...

Keeping an open mind without losing yours....

What's my opinion?....

Set your standards high....

Morals to guide you....

Living by principles....

*Discovering fundamental
Truths....*

Send out Your light and Your truth; let them guide me.
Let them lead me to Your holy mountain, to the place where You live.

PSALM 43:3 NLT

The world is moved along, not only by the mighty shoves of its heroes, but also by the aggregate of the tiny pushes of each honest worker.

HELEN KELLER

Who will influence you?

Choosing a mentor....

*Don't call just anybody
your hero....*

Spiritual life....

There are so many paths....

My experience in searching....

Discerning the Truth....

My child, don't lose sight of common sense and discernment.
Hang on to them, for they will refresh your soul.
They are like jewels on a necklace.

PROVERBS 3:21-22 NLT

Choose a job you love, and you will never have to work a day in your life.

Choosing your life's work....

Put your life into your work....

Making time for life outside of work....

Understanding true success....

Who do you think you are?....

Who do other people
think you are?....

Who does God think you are?

Living up to your potential....

What marvelous love the Father has extended to us! Just look at it—
we're called children of God! That's who we really are.

1 JOHN 3:1 THE MESSAGE

Allow your dreams a place in your prayers and plans. God-given dreams can help you move into the future He is preparing for you.

BARBARA JOHNSON

Live in the light of hope....

Make your wishes into prayers....

*Dream big and reach
for the stars....*

Sharing God's Word with You

Open your hearts to the love God instills....
God loves you tenderly. What He
gives you is not to be kept under
lock and key, but to be shared.

MOTHER TERESA

My life verse....

*When I found my
life verse....*

The special meaning it has for me....

Let the message about Christ, in all its richness, fill your lives....
Sing psalms and hymns and
spiritual songs to God with thankful hearts.

COLOSSIANS 3:16 NLT

I did not go through the Book. The Book went through me.

A. W. TOZER

My favorite book of the Bible....

I like using this version....

My plans to read through
the Bible....

Reading the Bible to others....

Words that comfort me....

When I am in need of encouragement, I turn to....

When I want to sing praises,
I look up this verse....

To offer thanks, I find this
special passage....

Even if it was written in Scripture long ago, you can be sure it's
written for us. God wants...His steady, constant calling and warm,
personal counsel in Scripture to come to characterize us,
keeping us alert for whatever He will do next.

ROMANS 15:4 THE MESSAGE

The Bible is not only a book which I can understand;
it is also a book which understands me.

EMILE CAILLET

Personal Bible study insights....

*Study helps I like to use when
I read my devotions....*

My prayer time alone or with a
prayer partner....

My favorite time of day to
read the Scriptures....

I love the Bible story about....

The Old Testament stories show me so much....

I am inspired by the
New Testament....

Finding gems and treasures
in my study....

Everyone will share the story of Your wonderful goodness;
they will sing with joy about Your righteousness.

PSALM 145:7 NLT

By reading of Scripture I am so renewed that all nature seems renewed around me and with me. The sky seems to be a purer, a cooler blue, the trees a deeper green,...and the whole world is charged with the glory of God.

THOMAS MERTON

The first verse I memorized...

When Scripture comes to mind....

My favorite way to memorize God's Word....

Praise time with God's Word....

When I'm singing praises....

I like to fill my worship time with...

He put a new song in my mouth, a song of praise to our God.
Many people will see this and worship Him. Then they will trust the Lord.

PSALM 40:3 NCV

It's Such a Grand Thing

Enjoy this extra section to write
anything you want. A letter to each
grandchild.... Your own poetry....
Favorite songs or verses....
Recipes to pass along....

If your baby is "beautiful and perfect, never cries or fusses, sleeps on schedule and burps on demand, an angel all the time," you're the grandma.

TERESA BLOOMINGDALE

Grandparents are similar to a piece of string—handy to have around and easily wrapped around the fingers of their grandchildren.

Surely, two of the most satisfying experiences in life must be
those of being a grandchild or a grandparent.

DONALD A. NORBERG

What a bargain grandchildren are! I give them my loose change, and they give me a million dollars worth of pleasure.

GENE PERRET

Grandmas don't just say "that's nice"—they reel back and roll their eyes and throw up their hands and smile. You get your money's worth out of grandmas.

HANNAH WHITHALL SMITH

....

....

....

....

....

....

....

....

....

....

....

....

*Grandmas hold our tiny hands
for just a little while,
but our hearts forever.*